HORSES

PAULA HAMMOND

This pocket edition first published in 2023

First published in a hardback edition in 2020

Copyright © 2023 Amber Books Ltd

Published by
Amber Books Ltd
United House
London N7 9DP
United Kingdom
www.amberbooks.co.uk
Instagram: amberbooksltd
Pinterest: amberbooksltd
Twitter: @amberbooks

ISBN: 978-1-83886-259-6

Project Editor: Sarah Uttridge
Designer: Jerry Williams
Picture Research: Terry Forshaw

Printed in China

Contents

Introduction

In the torch light, the animals painted onto the walls and ceilings appear to move. Flickering and dancing in the half-light, the 17,000-year-old cave paintings of Lascaux, France, tell the story of our enduring relationship with nature. And there, amongst the stylized images of bisons and bulls, stags and ibex, you'll find over 300 images of horses.

Our ancient ancestors hunted horses. Around 3500 BC the Botai people, who lived on the grasslands in what is now Kazakhstan, began to domesticate them – rearing horses for meat and milk. Then, suddenly, something changed. People began to see horses as more than food. Worn-down horse teeth have been found, suggesting that, around 5000 years ago, humans developed harnesses and riding bits. A thousand years later, images of horse-drawn carriages started appearing.

Horses gave humans the ability to travel further, faster – allowing them to connect and trade with other communities. It was a horse-fuelled revolution and it not only changed the world. It forged enduring bonds between humans and horses.

OPPOSITE:
The American Saddlebred is perhaps the archetypal horse: beautiful, lithe, spirited but gentle.

Types of Horses

If we could travel back in time 54 million years, there, grazing on the grasslands, we'd see small, dog-sized mammals, with hooves in place of claws. These ancient horses looked very different from their modern counterparts. In fact, horses as we would recognize them, only arrived on the scene around five million years ago. Horses belong to the family *Equidae*, which includes asses and zebra. Ponies aren't a separate species, but breeds of small horse.

From the tiny Falabellas to the massive Shires, these beautiful animals vary greatly in stature, strength and speed. Many of these differences are due to selective breeding. Over thousands of years, humans have crafted the horse into a tool, changing its body shape and size to suit our wants and whims.

Today, there are at least 350 different breeds. Modern 'hot-blooded' light horse breeds have been bred for riding and racing, with an emphasis on physical qualities that increase speed, stamina and agility. The 'cold-blooded' heavy horses have been bred for pulling and carrying loads, with body shapes that emphasize strength and endurance.

It's a sad truth that, at times, we've used and abused this incredible creature. But we've also appreciated it for its grace, strength and beauty. Ancient cultures, from the Indus Valley to Bronze Age Britain, viewed the horse as a sacred animal, and horse cults and horse worship were widespread. Today, while many horses are still viewed as working animals, many more are kept as pets – cared for, and loved.

OPPOSITE:
When is a Horse a Pony?
Shetland Ponies generally measure less than 14.2 hands tall, with short legs and stocky barrels (the distance between the legs). Miniature horses, like the eight-hand high Falabellas, aren't classed as ponies because they have a more horse-like body shape.

High Class Horse

While the term thoroughbred is used to mean any pedigree horse, Thoroughbreds are a distinct breed, famous for their speed and agility. Throughbreds are most often used in racing or show-jumping and can trace their lineage to horses bred in England during the 17th and 18th centuries.

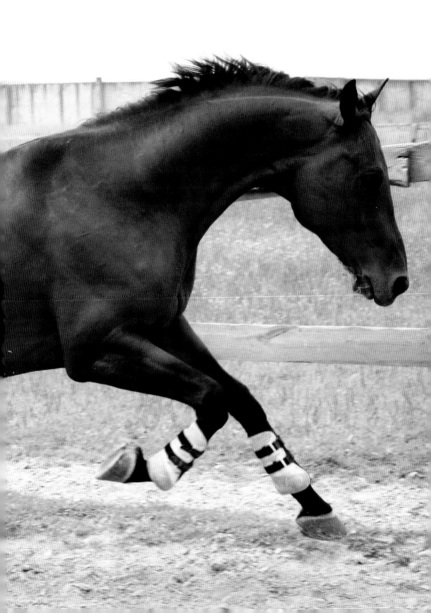

RIGHT:

The Horse Nation

North America's magnificent Mustangs are descended from horses brought to the continent by the Spanish Conquistadores. Before horses arrived in North America, native peoples travelled everywhere on foot or by canoe. Horses brought rapid change and were called, by some tribes, the Horse Nation, reflecting respect and a sense of kinship.

FOLLOWING PAGES:

Home on the Range

Feral Mustangs are considered by many be a living symbol – and link to – the old, Wild West. More than half of all free-roaming Mustangs can be found in Nevada, with sizeable herds also found in parts of California, Montana, Oregon, Utah and Wyoming.

ABOVE:

**A Horse of
a Different Colour**

Horse terminology
includes special names
for almost every part of
the horse's anatomy. This
South African Boerperd
horse is a light chestnut
colour, which is known
as strawberry roan. Roan
is the name given to any
animal that has a mix of
white and coloured hair
in its coat.

OPPOSITE:

Spot the Difference

These distinctive spotted
horses were a favourite
of Idaho's Nez Perce
tribe, who regarded
them as hardier and
better-natured than
single-coloured horses.
European settlers referred
to the horses as 'A
Palouse' or Appaloosa in
reference to the nearby
Palouse River – and the
name stuck.

Ancient Ways
The Kazakhs of the Asian steppe were one of the earliest peoples to domesticate horses, and tribesmen in the region still live side-by-side with their horses. Famous for their hardiness and stamina, Kazakh horses are also eaten, reflecting a tradition that probably goes back thousands of years.

Little Big Horse
These small horses have been part of life in the
Scottish Shetlands since the Bronze Age. Today,
Shetland ponies are popular pets but, historically, these
powerful animals worked hard, pulling ploughs and
hauling peat. During the Industrial Revolution they
were used in coal mines and many spent their entire
lives underground.

Putting on Airs

Lipizzaners have been immortalized in film, book and song as white horses. However, they are grey – born with a black coat that lightens with age. Lipizzaner horses are trained to do performances, involving hopping and standing on their hind-legs. These movements are called 'airs above the ground'.

Standing Tall

Russian Dons average between 15.2–16.2 hands tall. Named after the region of treeless plains surrounding the Don River, these are long-legged, muscular equines.

Strong and Fast

Dons were used by the Cossacks as cavalry horses. During the 1812 war against Napoleon, the Don's exceptional stamina enabled the Cossacks to chase the invaders out of Russia. They remained a vital part of Russia's armed forces until cavalry units were replaced by tanks after World War I.

Horse Power

Working horses like this Schleswig are known as cold-bloods due to their gentle temperaments. Bred to be hard-working, and to carry and pull heavy loads, Schleswigs provided the literal horse-power on German farms and for the timber industry until the large-scale mechanization of agriculture in the 1950s.

Weights and Measures

Britain's version of the Schleswig is the Shire horse. Individual Shires have been record-breakers. On average, males measure around 17.2 hands – mares (females) can be up to a hand shorter. The tallest recorded Shire measured 21.2 hands. This equine giant, known as Mammoth, also weighed an incredible 1524kg (3360lbs).

A Real Work Horse

This magnificent Soviet Heavy Draft horse is a result of generations of specialist breeding designed to produce an animal for a specific type of work. These powerfully-built beasts have short, powerful legs, with strong joints and broad hooves. This makes them ideal for pulling heavy weights in difficult conditions.

OPPOSITE:

Riding into History

Morgan horses have played an integral role in the history of America. The great-grandaddy of these agile riding horses was Figure, owned by a horse-breeder called Justin Morgan in 1780s. The horse's descendants became one of the USA's most enduring breeds, serving in the cavalry on both sides in the Civil War.

ABOVE:

America's Horse

American Quarter Horses range in size from 14 to 16 hands and weigh between 431–544kg (950–1200lbs). They are compact and powerful, with strong haunches. This allows them to make sudden, fast turns. Combined with their instinctive 'cattle-sense' this has traditionally made them a popular choice with cattle herders.

A Horse for a Knight...
and a Night

A French medieval tale
mentioned how the
Count of Perche's horses
were bred to support the
weight of an armoured
knight. Later, Percheron
horses were used to pull
wagons and coaches, with
light-coloured horses
preferred as they were
easier to see in the dark.

ABOVE:
The Spoils of War
According to legend, the lineage of the Percheron horse dates back to AD 732, when Charles Martel defeated the Moorish army at Poitiers. He claimed the enemy's horses as spoils of war, and many ended up in the Perche district of Normandy, where they inter-bred with local horses.

OPPOSITE TOP:
A Smooth Ride
Despite their name, the Rocky Mountain horse originated in Kentucky's Appalachian Mountains. When most horses trot, one diagonal pair of feet rises as another pair falls. Rocky Mountain horses have an ambling gait, where one foot is always on the ground. This gives a smoother ride and makes them popular trail horses.

OPPOSITE BOTTOM:
Ancient Stock
Przewalski's horses are perhaps the world's only remaining truly wild horse. Natives of the grassland steppes of central Asia, they live in family groups usually containing one adult male, 1–3 adult females, and their offspring. Genetically, they are similar to the horses domesticated by the Botai people.

Hardy Horses

These small and shaggy equines may look like ponies, but they are Mongolian horses. In Mongolia, there are more horses than people, and most roam wild, fending for themselves until needed. They are so hardy they require very little food and, despite little structured care, they can live to between 20–40 years old.

Golden Horses

Thanks to their coats' metallic sheen, Akhal-Teke horses are also known as 'golden horses'. Named after the Teke tribe from the Akhal oasis, in Turkmenistan, they are famous for their speed and endurance. These strikingly handsome beasts may be one of the world's oldest and rarest horse breeds.

OPPOSITE:
Made to Measure
Orlov Trotters were first bred in the 1770s by Count Orlov, who wanted a horse with enough stamina to tolerate Russia's extreme climate, and a long-stride for easy riding on the country's terrible roads. To get these qualities he selectively bred Arabian, Pure Spanish and English Thoroughbred horses.

ABOVE:
Sporting Spots
Tarpan are a Danish horse breed, famous for their bold and unusual coat colours. They typically measure between 15–16 hands, although some are pony size. Coat patterns range from solid colours to full leopard-style spots – and this remains the most popular colour.

Winning Tactics
Inward turning ears are the most notable feature of India's majestic Marwari horse. The Rajputs used Marwari horses in battle, where they were trained to fight sword-wielding enemies riding elephants. The cavalry riders fashioned false trunks for their horses, making them appear to be baby elephants, which the adults would not attack.

RIGHT:
Walk the Walk
Despite looking like a draught horse, this Friesian is a graceful mover. Here, it is seen doing 'the Spanish' walk, in which it raises each foreleg, in turn, in an exaggerated manner.

OPPOSITE TOP:
Celebrity Clydesdales
Clydesdale draught horses are perhaps Scotland's most high-profile heavy horse breed. A team of eight Clydesdales are used by the Budweiser brewery on promotional tours. Clydesdales are also used as drum horses by Britain's Household Cavalry, and are a popular sight in parades or on official state occasions.

OPPOSITE BELOW:
Gentle Giants
Measuring between 15–16 hands tall and weighing between 700–750kg (1543–1653lbs), Dutch Draft horses are muscular and heavily-built. Despite their size, they have a calm disposition which – now that they are rarely used as work horses – has made them popular guests at country shows.

Rare Beauties
Suffolk Punch horses are always a chestnut colour
(which is spelled 'chesnut' in horse-breeding circles).
Developed by English farmers to pull ploughs through
Suffolk's clay-heavy soil, the 'Punch' in their name
is indicative of their toughness and stamina. Once
common, these beautiful animals are now endangered.

OPPOSITE:

An Ancient Breed
The horses of the
Camargue are indigenous
to the marshlands
of southern France.
Sometimes called 'sea
horses' because of their
affinity for water, these
characterful horses may
be one of the oldest
breeds in the world.
Today, they live in semi-
feral, managed herds
in the Camargue
Regional Park.

ABOVE:

Resetting the Balance
Konik is Polish for 'small
horse', and these tough
equines rarely grow
larger than 12.3–13.3
hands tall. Koniks are
believed to be descended
from the extinct Tarpan
and some herds have
been selectively bred to
recreate a Tarpan-type
horse as part of plans
to restore grassland and
wetland eco-systems.

Reining Specialist

The Mexican Azteca is a relatively new breed, dating from 1972. Bred from Andalusian, American Quarter Horses and Mexican Criollos, the Azteca was intended to reflect the type of horse brought to Latin America by the Conquistadors. The Azteca is agile and intelligent, excelling at the type of intricate reining manoeuvres required in dressage, on ranches and playing polo.

Mountain Mounts
Many of the villages
in the Austrian Tyrol
mountain region, where
Haflinger horses originate,
are accessible only by
narrow paths – making
such small, sure-footed
animals vital. Dating
back to the Middle Ages,
Haflingers are chestnut
in colour.

Ice Age Animals?
Norwegian Fjord horses
are small and dexterous.
Looking remarkably
similar to horses seen
painted on Ice Age cave
walls, this is an ancient
breed, related to the wild
Przewalski' horse. These
mini draught horses have
been in Norway for at
least 4000 years.

A Basque Breed
The Basques of France
and Spain believe that
these feral horses are
descended from breeds
used by Europe's
Magdalenian people, who
lived around 11,000–
17,000 years ago. Standing
between 11.1–14.2 hands
high, pure-breed Pottoks
are now endangered.

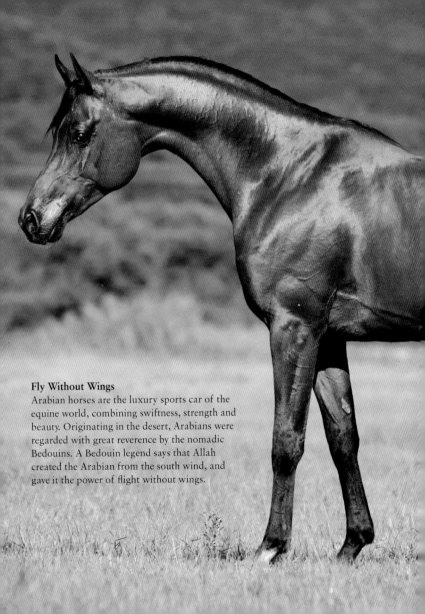

Fly Without Wings
Arabian horses are the luxury sports car of the
equine world, combining swiftness, strength and
beauty. Originating in the desert, Arabians were
regarded with great reverence by the nomadic
Bedouins. A Bedouin legend says that Allah
created the Arabian from the south wind, and
gave it the power of flight without wings.

OPPOSITE:

Bred for Success

These striking draught horses were bred from a cross between the heavy Belgian Ardennes and the smaller North Swedish Horse. The aim was to develop a breed which was strong but compact in size, for work on farms and hauling timber. They remain one of Sweden's most popular horses.

ABOVE:

On the Trail

As its name suggests, the Tennessee Walker, or Walking Horse, is a popular trail-riding horse. On average a walking horse can travel at 6.4–12.9km/h (4–8mph). The Tennessee is known for its exceptionally smooth 'running walk', which it can do at speeds of 16–32km/h (10–20mph).

FOLLOWING PAGES:

Bright and Fiery

Horses arrived in Australia with the British fleet in 1788. Their feral descendants are called Brumbies, possibly from the Aboriginal word 'baroomby', meaning wild.

Horse Anatomy

Horses are herbivores and, like many prey species, they have evolved to be fast and strong – able to survive in environments where food is scarce and the predators are plentiful. Over millions of years, these hardy creatures slowly began to adapt to environmental pressures. The long bones in their lower legs became fused, making them faster. Three toes became one sturdy hoof. The joint connecting the hoof to the bones of the ankles and lower leg developed to be both a shock-absorber and a spring, to help propel them forward at speed.

However, studies have shown that, once they became domesticated, horse anatomy underwent even more dramatic changes as humans selectively bred horses to emphasize desirable temperaments and traits. Their muscle bulk grew. Their limbs became even stronger and longer. Their hearts became larger, while their balance and intelligence increased.

In the past, such traits were a necessity for a working horse. A muscular animal, with a larger heart, is more athletic and has more stamina. Better balance and longer legs make a horse easier to ride. Eventually, though, horses proved not just their worth but their value. Stud books were started to prove the lineage of particularly successful breeds and specialist words were developed to tell a horse-fancier everything they need to know about an animal.

OPPOSITE:
Blazes, Snips, Stars and Stripes
Horse-breeders have terms for different types of horse colourings and markings. A broad white stripe, from the forehead to the nose, is called a blaze. A 'snip' is any small white patch, near the nostrils. A 'star' is a small, white patch on the forehead. A 'stripe' is a thinner blaze.

The Name Game

Various terms are applied to horses, depending on their age and sex. Male horses who haven't been castrated (gelded) are called stallions. Females are known as mares. A foal is under a year old. A filly is a female under four years of age. A colt is a male under four years that hasn't been gelded.

Listen Up!

Prey species spend a large part of their day watching and listening for predators – and ancient horses evolved to be ever-alert to danger. Their ears can move independently of one other, and are able to rotate up to 180 degrees. This allows the horse to listen for danger without, potentially, turning its back on a predator.

Many Colours

While most horses' eyes
are dark brown, blue,
green and amber irises are
not especially rare. Blue
eyes are more likely to
occur in horses who are
white or have prominent
white markings but, just
as in humans, genetics –
and the eye colour
of the horse's sires –
plays a part.

OPPOSITE:

Extra Protection

Horses have a partial
third eyelid called a
nictating membrane. This
is pinkish or transparent
in colour and located
near the tear duct. It
often goes unnoticed until
it slides, horizontally,
across the eye to protect
the eye from damage.
Such membranes are
common in reptiles and
birds, but unusual in
mammals.

Horse Hair

A horse's mane grows from the poll (the area behind the ears) to its withers (the distinctive bump where the shoulder blades lie). Truly wild horses have short, more erect manes. Domesticated horses have longer manes, which have been selectively bred to be visually appealing to humans.

FOLLOWING PAGES:
Dressing for Dressage

In the past, horses' manes were braided to stop them getting caught in foliage while they were working. Today, they're generally braided for show. Button or rosette braids, as shown here, are a style of mane braiding that has become increasingly popular for competition and dressage events.

The Horse's Whiskers
These thin, wiry hairs around the horse's muzzle and eyes are called vibrissae. Vibrissae are incredibly sensitive, picking up and relaying information about the world in the same way that a cat's whiskers do. They help inform a horse about what's happening in the blind spots in front of its face and underneath its nose.

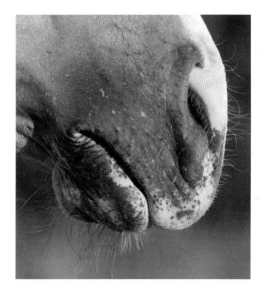

A Flexible Tool
An equine's tongue is a powerful tool: muscular and flexible. Once food is in the mouth, small bumps on the tongue, called papillae, help the grass stick to the tongue, enabling the animal to grind its food against the roof of its mouth.

Nose Nuances
Horse-breeders often say that they can tell a horse's mood by looking at its nostrils. Flared nostrils when a horse is at rest may mean fear or curiosity – it's exploring its surroundings by having a good sniff!

Heads Up!

While most herbivores have short necks that are held downwards for grazing grass, horses' heads are very flexible and are held in a much more upright position. To do this requires a lot of muscles – over a hundred, in fact. This represents six per cent of the horse's entire body mass.

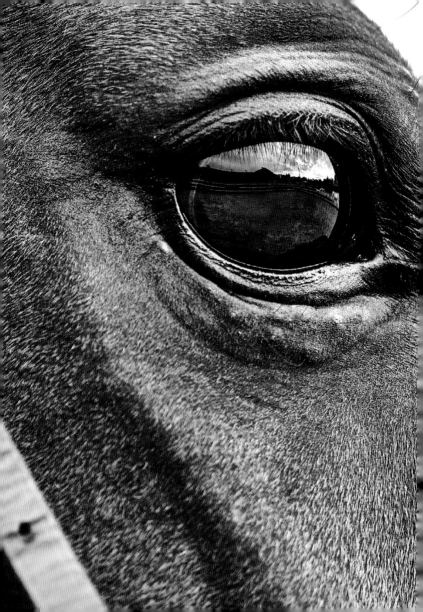

The Eyes Have It
Horses' eyes are amongst the largest of any land mammal. They can see almost 350 degrees in any direction and, like many prey animals, are very sensitive to sudden movements. Their night vision is better than ours, but they take longer to adjust to sudden changes in brightness.

A Winter Coat

The trigger for horses to begin growing their longer winter coats is diminishing daylight, rather than colder weather. The shorter days cause the horse's body to increase production of the hormone melatonin, which spurs coat growth. As daylight hours increase in the spring, melatonin production drops and long coats begin to shed.

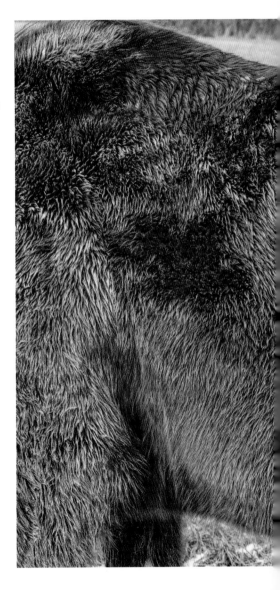

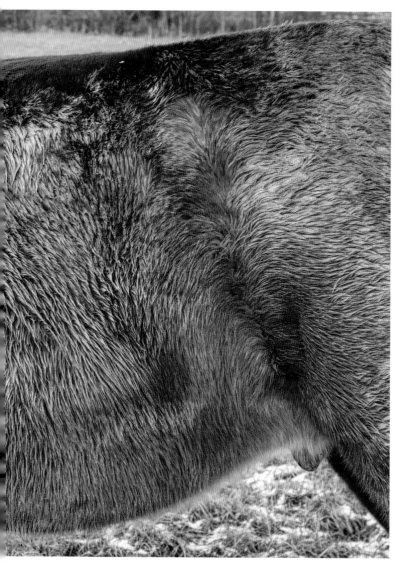

PREVIOUS PAGE LEFT:
A Sign of Trouble
At a week old, this foal already has a shaggy tail. By the time it is fully grown, the tail will have become a useful tool for swatting away biting and stinging insects. At this early age, excessive tail movements may also be an indicator of a foal in a distressed state.

PREVIOUS PAGE RIGHT:
Furry Feet
The long hair around a horse's feet is known as feathering. In ponies and heavy horse breeds, like this one, these long, silky hairs may cover the lower legs and hooves entirely. These hairs were developed to shield the horses' lower legs from cuts and grazes caused by stones and foliage.

LEFT:
Grazing Not Gorging
To stay healthy, horses should ideally be fed on the sort of diet they would have in the wild: grass, with lots of fresh, clean water. Horses have relatively small stomachs for their size, and have evolved to eat little and often.

Feeding and Fighting

An adult stallion should have around 40–42 teeth. At the front of the mouth are 12 chisel-like incisors for cutting grass. Flat molars at the back of the mouth are used to grind food. Some males have sharp canine 'fighting teeth', used to compete for mares during breeding season.

LEFT:

Powering the Engine

This beautiful Pinto Arabian is every inch an athlete. The engine that powers this incredible creature is its heart. Equine hearts are very efficient – moving oxygenated blood around the body to fuel the muscles. Horse hearts can beat at 30 beats-per-minute at rest, and up to 240 beats-per-minute when galloping.

BELOW:

A Vital Link

A horse's fore-legs carry the majority of its weight – up to 60 per cent. Its hind-legs supply the power. The lump on the leg, called the fetlock, is a hinge joint. This joint acts as a shock-absorber and energy transmitter, allowing horses to jump and gallop.

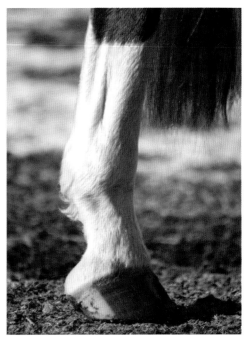

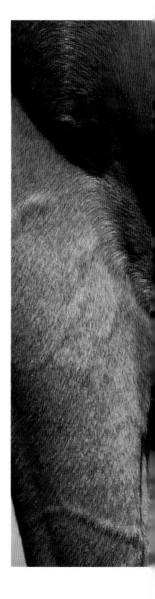

RIGHT:

Powerful Pectorals

Horses don't have a collarbone to connect their front limbs to the body. Instead, strong muscles tether the inside of their shoulder blades to the rib cage. These pectoral muscles act like a sling and suspend the chest between the horse's two front limbs, creating this characteristic inverted v-shape.

NEXT PAGE TOP LEFT:

Frogs and Horses

The v-shaped area of spongy tissue (shown) is called a frog. It works like a shock-absorber, as well as giving the horse traction on slippy ground. Amazingly, it also acts like a second heart, pushing blood back up the leg when the frog has pressure on it.

NEXT PAGE MIDDLE LEFT:

Boots and Shoes

Ancient cultures recognized the damage that could be caused to horses' feet from over-work. It is believed that Romans and some Northern European tribes shod their horses in leather boots. The first evidence of metal horseshoes – made from bronze – comes from an Etruscan tomb dating around 400 BC.

NEXT PAGE BOTTOM LEFT:

Professional Foot Care

By the Middle Ages, iron horse shoes were common. Today, they are usually made from steel and are nailed or glued to the hoof by professional farriers. The nails are shaped so that they bend outwards, thereby avoiding damage to the sensitive inner part of the foot.

NEXT PAGE RIGHT:

Daily Care

A horse's care routine should involve regular foot check-ups. Hoof picks should be used, daily, to pick out grit. Hoof oil, applied every other day, is needed to stop hooves splitting and cracking.

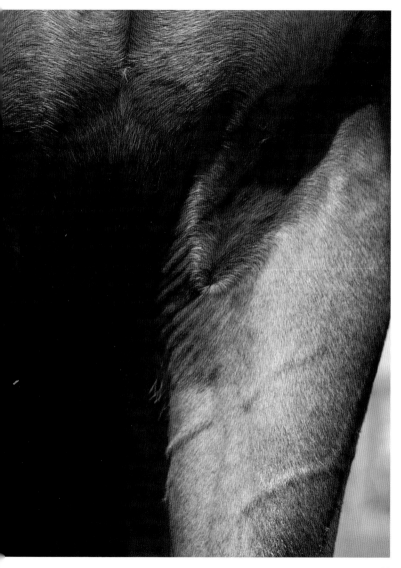

ABOVE TOP:

Why Wear Shoes?

Wild horses don't need shoes because they spend their time travelling across dry grasslands in search of food. Such migrations are enough to keep their hooves worn smooth. Domesticated horses may live in colder, wetter environments, with plenty of potential hazards underfoot.

ABOVE BOTTOM:

A Bad Break

Without protection, hooves can wear unevenly, split or become infected. Cracks – where there is a break in the hoof wall – are known as grass cracks or sand cracks, depending on their location. This type of damage often occurs in unshod horses, when the hoof wall gets damaged as it hits the ground.

OPPOSITE:

Small Horse, Big Commitment

Sadly, the popularity of miniature horses, like this American Palomino, has resulted in an increase in animal neglect. Small horses are often viewed as cute accessories that are abandoned when their owners realize that they require the same care and attention as a fully-grown horse.

Lift-Off!

In 1878, Eadweard Muybridge produced a series of photographs to answer the question: do all four of a horse's legs ever leave the ground at the same time? The answer was yes. At a gallop, as its

hind-legs move towards
its front-legs, the horse is
effectively airborne.

**Healthy Hair,
Healthy Horse**

In addition to cleaning a horse's coat, regular grooming stimulates the sebaceous gland. This produces sebum, a natural oil, that coats each strand of hair. Sebum provides a protective barrier for both the skin and hair, helping to repel water and prevent ticks, fungus or infections from taking hold.

Primitive Marks

This distinctive dark line running down this horse's back is called a dorsal stripe. Such marks are found in primitive breeds. All dun-coloured horses have a dorsal stripe and those with a chestnut base-colour are thought to be descended from some of the most ancient breeds. Duns with a black- base colour also exist.

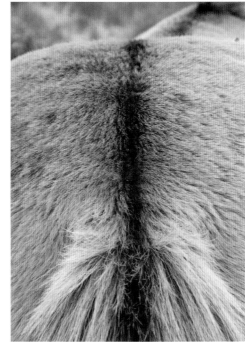

PREVIOUS PAGE TOP:
A Painful Process?
Some horse owners 'pull' their horse's mane, using a small metal comb to pluck out sections of hair to make it look thinner and neater.

PREVIOUS PAGE BOTTOM & RIGHT:
A Tale of a Tail
A horse's tail is divided into two parts. The 'dock' is the muscular area that sits over the coccyx (tail bone). The skirt refers to the long hairs that fall below the dock. Traditionally some work horses had their tails 'docked' (cut off), but this is now considered unnecessary and cruel.

Working Horses

O ur equine companions were the literal work-horses that powered the Industrial Revolution. They took our ancestors on journeys of exploration. They allowed settlers to travel to far-flung places, pulling wagons across thousands of miles through unforgiving terrain. They were used as an instrument of war. The speed and flexibility of the horse allowed armies to cover vast distances quickly, to dominate and subdue their neighbours. Horses have even became skilled entertainers, wowing audiences in circuses, at rodeos and country shows with demonstrations of agility and precision.

The importance of horses to human society is reflected in the sheer number of everyday words and phrases that reference them. The measure of an engine's performance is still made in horsepower.

To 'take something in your stride' is a horse racing term meaning that you're doing well. To 'chomp at the bit' means to be eager to begin, and references the part of the horse's tack (actually called a mullen) that fits inside the horse's mouth and helps the rider control its actions.

Through much of human history, where there was work to be done, the horse was co-opted to the task. Today, even horses who are kept as pets must still work hard for their hay.

OPPOSITE:
Testing Times
Competitions, such as this three-day event at Moscow's Equestrian Centre, are designed to challenge the skills of both horse and rider. Competitors are tested across three different disciplines: cross-country (shown), dressage and showjumping. The secret to success is the bond between the horse and its rider.

PREVIOUS PAGES:
Dressed to Impress
These officers are members of Rome's Carabinieri Mounted Regiment. While they undertake many of the usual police activities, including street patrols and riot control, they are famous for their performance of the 'horse carousel', which reenacts the Carabinieri's charge at the Battle of Pastrengo in 1848.

LEFT:

A Real Work-Horse
Knabstrupper horses are regarded as a calm and friendly breed, with a good work-ethic. They aren't as strong as draught horses, so were mostly used for pulling light carriages or pleasure carts (a type of small, four-wheeled carriage). They continue to be popular show-horses.

Pulling more than their Weight

During her coronation in 1533 England's Queen Mary need six horses to drag her state coach through the thick London mud. Even on good roads, ceremonial carriages can weigh several tons, which is why this example, outside the Winter Palace in St Petersburg, is pulled by draught horses.

Demanding Work

Police horses have perhaps the most demanding job of all working horses. To do it well, they must learn not to behave like horses at all! They need to be focused, ignore loud noises and sudden movements, and be calm in situations that would make most animals nervous.

OPPOSITE:

Poetry in Motion

When a horse jumps, there are five distinct stages: approach, takeoff, flight, landing and recovery. Co-operation between the horse and its rider is vital at every stage. The wrong move from a rider can unbalance the horse and result in a a painful landing for both parties.

ABOVE:

A Cross-Country Challenge

Cross-country trails are more than a test of a horse's speed and agility. They are a test of endurance. A standard cross-country course is approximately 6–6.4km (2¾–4 miles) long and includes 24–36 obstacles that have to be jumped or crossed.

ABOVE:

Born Riders

Mongol children begin riding almost before they can walk and start horse racing as young as six years old. No wonder, then, that American academic Elizabeth Kendall, in her 1913 travelogue *A Wayfarer in China*, said: 'The Mongol without his pony is only half a Mongol, but with his pony he is as good as two men.'

RIGHT:

War-Winners

The great Mongol leader Genghis Khan (c. 1162–1227) credited his success in war to horses. Mongol cavalry were said to prefer riding lactating mares, because they would be able to drink the milk while on campaign. They also drank horse blood if rations were scarce.

Snow Horses

The annual winter horse race in Kars, northern Turkey, is a colourful spectacle – popular with both locals and tourists. The horses are dressed in traditional harnesses and work in teams of two, pulling a box-like wooden sled through the snow and across the frozen Lake Çıldır.

LEFT:

A Tradition Continues
In most parts of the world trucks have taken the place of horse power. However, horses are still used in areas where machinery would be impractical. Here, in the plantations of Vattavada, India, horses are often used to transport harvests through the narrow tracks and thickly-packed foliage.

FOLLOWING PAGES:

Ceremonial Duties
Horse-mounted cavalry units were once the backbone of every army. In the United States' Army, there are now just seven horse-mounted units. Their duties are mainly ceremonial. Here, mounted troops lead the Presidential Inauguration Parade in Washington, D.C., after the 2013 swearing-in ceremony.

LEFT:
A Legendary Team
Employed in cattle
drives and in day-to-day
work around the ranch,
cowboys and cowgirls
are almost mythic figures
in America's 'wild west'.
Working with a good
stock horse – strong and
not too large – their work
is much the same today as
it was in the 19th century.

FOLLOWING PAGES:
Sized for Success
In horse racing, the rider
needs to be just as much
of a specialist as the
horse. Jockeys have to
be light enough not to
slow down the horse, but
strong enough to control
it. The average jockey is
1.6m (5ft 2in) tall and
weighs 53.5kg (118lbs).

Cheap Alternatives?
During the Great Depression, when petrol was scarce, horses were used to pull modified cars called Hoover wagons. Today, they still provide transport for poorer families, such as here in Brazil.

Popular Attractions
Samsun in Turkey is well known for its fanciful, open-topped carriages, called *fayton*, which take tourists on drives along the coastal roads. Concerns about animal welfare has led to some parts of Turkey banning horse-drawn carriages on traffic-choked roads.

**Old Tradition,
New Rules**
Horse-drawn carriages in Central Park, Manhattan, have been a popular tourist attraction for 150 years. Regulations now prevent horses from working if the weather is too hot or too cold, and there are strict limits on the number of people each carriage can accommodate.

Speeding Through the Snow
In Romania, heavy snowfall in the Transylvanian
Alps often means that the only way to get around in
the winter is by horse-drawn sled. Draught horses,
which are used to the mountain terrain and familiar
with the routes, make hard work in these difficult
conditions look easy.

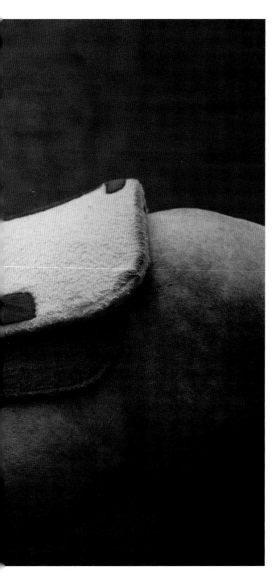

PREVIOUS PAGES:

A Winning Combination
Lucy Davis rides her gelding, Barron, during the team jumping on day 11 of the Rio 2016 Olympic Games. Lucy and Barron helped win a silver medal for the USA equestrian team. Barron is a Belgian Warmblood – a breed famous for their jumping abilities.

LEFT:

Healing Horses
It's long been acknowledged that interacting with animals can have a beneficial impact on mental health. Learning to win the trust of such a large animal is often an emotional and healing experience, and equine-assisted therapy has proved to be especially effective in treating anxiety and stress.

LEFT:

An Historic Trail

A cattle drive near Eidsvold Station, Queensland, Australia. Eidsvold was founded in 1848 and is one of the region's oldest homesteads. Climate change and falling cattle prices have meant that commercial drives are now a rare event, but the Eidsvold Charity Cattle Drive continues the tradition.

ABOVE:

Connecting to the Past

The Eidsvold Charity Cattle Drive has not only raised money for good causes, but given a huge boost to tourism in Queensland. At each overnight stop along the drive, owners of properties tell their stories and give an insight into an age when horse and cattle dominated the area.

A Special Status

In the band of the British Household Cavalry, the drum horse has a special status. These Shires carry the rank of major and are senior to all other animals in the army. During training, time must be taken to get the horse used to the sound and vibrations of the drum being played.

A Test of Skill

Dressage is a French term that loosely translates as 'training'. Its roots go back to the treatise 'On Horsemanship' written by the Ancient Greek general Xenophon (c. 430–354 BC). Modern dressage is a showcase for the skills of rider and horse, who are dressed simply but formally.

Horses' Easter
Bulgaria's mounted police parade as part of the St Todor's Day celebrations. Todor's or Theodore's Day is also known as 'Horses' Easter'. According to legend, this is when the saint rides out on his white horse to beg God to bring spring. The festival is also marked by traditional horse races known as *kushii*.

ABOVE:
First Responders
In the 19th century, mounted police units, such as this one in Jakarta, Indonesia, were used because an officer on horseback was able to respond much more quickly than on foot. Today, police horses are used mainly for crowd control due to their imposing size.

RIGHT:
Picture Perfect
Mounted police units are popular tourist attractions. This police officer patrols the Souq Waqif in Doha – the Qatari capital's largest old-style market. He wears traditional riding gear and is mounted on a white, Arabian horse – a scene that would look perfect on any picture postcard!

LEFT:

National Treasure or Eco-Disaster?

Horses became extinct in North America between 13,000–11,000 years ago. Feral Mustangs are descended from horses brought to the continent by the Spanish. As such, conservation groups are divided on how best to manage these herds, which can damage desert ecosystems with overgrazing.

ABOVE:

National Icons

Argentina's gauchos are ranchers and cattle-herders and, like American cowboys, they have become symbolic of a mythic age. Jose Hernandez's poem 'Martin Fierro' tells of a gaucho who is forced to give up his way of life. The epic represents gauchos as icons of freedom and independence.

143

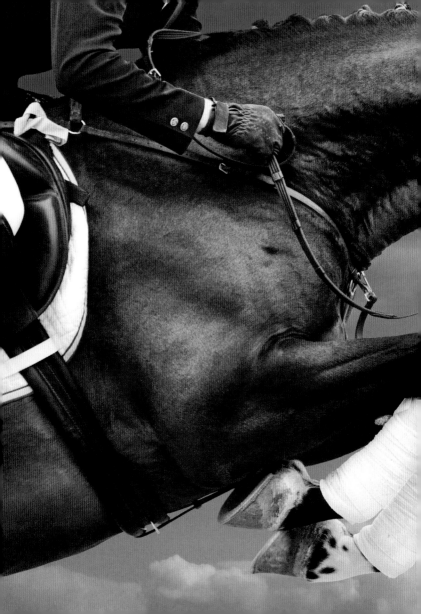

Slow and Steady

During eventing competitions, riders deliberately slow their horses as they approach an obstacle. This gives the horse time to judge the height of the obstacle. The faster a horse approaches a jump, the greater the likelihood of a fall, which is why steeplechases can be so dangerous.

A Reliable Partner

Italy's cowboys are known as the *butteri* and their horse of choice is the Maremmano (which is also known as the Tuscan horse). Due to the animal's strength and adaptability, especially over rough terrain, this is the same breed preferred by the Italian mounted police.

ABOVE:
Heavy Horses, Heavy Work
The Shire Horse Society's stud book dates the modern Shire horse to the 1770s but draught horses have been part of British life since the Middle Ages. These 'Great Horses' once carried knights into battle. After the arrival of gunpowder, which made horses impractical in warfare, they were co-opted for farm work.

OPPOSITE:
Urban and Rural
A Shire horse working fields somewhere in England as part of an historical event, to spotlight traditional farming practices. However, from the 18th century to the 1920s, Shire horses were a common sight in urban areas too, pulling the wagons that delivered coal and collected rubbish.

FOLLOWING PAGES:
Riding Out!
The Royal Canadian Mounted Police – known as 'Mounties' – are arguably the world's most famous mounted police force. These days, horses are only used on special occasions, such as The Musical Ride, which tours Canada annually raising money for charity. The Ride involves horse and rider performing drills set to music.

Timeless Trails
In Montana, USA, moving cattle from winter to summer pastures is still a necessity, and cowboys work in much the same way as they would have done 100 years ago. Increasingly ranches like this also offer the 'cowboy experience' to holidaymakers yearning to experience a simpler life.

LEFT:

Horses for Courses

This eight-horse hitch arrangement includes 'leaders' (in front), 'wheelers' (closest to the carriage) and 'swing horses' (in the middle). Wheelers should be the heaviest and strongest of the team, as they are always pulling. Swing horses need to be calm and well-balanced, while leaders should be well-trained.

ABOVE:

Horse in Harness

Where a carriage or buggy is pulled by a single horse, it is harnessed between two shafts. The shafts allow the 'pull' to be evenly distributed so that the carriage isn't dragged to the left or right. The harness allows the driver to control the horse directions.

Sharing the Load
A three-abreast formation is popular with farmers, for the simple reason that three horses can pull more and will tire less quickly. The standard harness configuration for a Russian *troika* is also three abreast. The horse in the middle trots, while those on the outside move at a faster canter.

The Nation's Favourite
Sweden has more than 360,000 horses, which equates to around 39 horses for every 1000 inhabitants. Most horses in Sweden are ridden for pleasure but some, such as shown here, attract tourists to historic farms.

Team Work
Two horses, harnessed together to pull a carriage or wagon, are known as a 'pair' or a 'team'. A 'tandem' is a pair of horses that are hitched, one in front of the other, rather than side-by-side. A pair of heavy draught horses can easily pull over two tons in weight.

Military Parade, Moscow, 2016
Drawn by a pair of horses and manned by soldiers in historical uniforms, a machine gun carriage (*tachanka*) takes part in a military parade in Moscow's Red Square. The event was to commemorate the 75th anniversary of the Red Army's defence of the city during World War II.

FOLLOWING PAGES:
Pulling their Weight
From December to early April, visitors to Canada's Lake Louise can experience picturesque sled rides – sometimes on the frozen waters of the lake itself. Canadian horses may be pony-sized but they are hardy beasts who grow thick coats in the winter and have hard hooves that rarely need shoes.

PREVIOUS PAGES:
Turning the Clocks Back
Using horses for hauling timber dates back almost 10,000 years. By the 1980s the practice had almost completely died out. However, an awareness of the damage caused by heavy machinery, and a call for more sustainable timber and land-use, has increasingly made horse-logging the environmental choice.

LEFT:
Bare-Backed Bravos
Italy's world-famous Palio di Siena horse race is held twice a year, on 2 July and 16 August. Unlike most horse races, the competitors ride bare-backed. The race happens in the Piazza del Campo in the centre of historic Siena, where riders must complete three laps.

A Calming Influence

Originating in the Normandy region of France – which is famous for its horse-breeding – Norman Cobs are medium-sized draught horses. Originally used for pulling mail or artillery wagons, this breed is popular in carriage racing and pleasure-riding, thanks to its calm disposition.

ABOVE:

Mutual Trust

Combined-driving is a sport that tests both the horse
and the driver's stamina. Successful competitors must
be able to work well together – and mutual trust is
vital. The competition includes a marathon stage which
takes the horse through numerous 'hazards', such as
shown here.

LEFT:

Regular Check-Ups

The marathon or cross-country stage of combined-
driving competitions can be stressful, tiring and
potentially dangerous – with obstacles, such as water
traps, gates and slopes, all part of the course. Such
trials therefore include mandatory stops to allow vets
to check the health of the horses.

Airs and Graces

Vienna's Spanish Riding School specializes in the training of Lipizzaner horses. The name comes from the Spanish horses who were the progenitors of the Lipizzaner breed. Here, a horse and its trainer demonstrate a capriole, where the horse jumps straight up and kicks out with its hind legs.

OPPOSITE:

A Thoroughbred Sport
In the sport of polo, horses are referred to as 'polo ponies'. Prior to 1899, the height limit for polo ponies was 13.2 hands. However, in the modern game, the name has no reflection on the size of the horse and large Throughbreds are the horse of choice for many professional players.

ABOVE TOP:

Spectacular Spectacles
These Throughbreds are being exercised on 'The Gallops' at Newmarket, in England. Gallops are tracks used to train horses between race meetings. These training sessions are unfenced and free to watch, although 1.5m (5ft) of horse flesh, thundering past at speed, is best viewed at a distance!

ABOVE BOTTOM:

The Slower the Better?
According to *Guinness World Records*, the fastest recorded horse speed is 70.76km/h (43.97mph). However, it is rarely the fastest horse that wins the race. Go too fast, too early, and you'll quickly tire – allowing your rivals to pass you on the home stretch.

Faster and Faster
Specialist breeding and changes in riding styles means
that the average winning time for a six-furlong race
has been cut by more than a second in the last 15 years.
A horse, today, would beat a horse from the 1990s by
seven horse lengths. (A horse length is approximately
2.4m/8ft.)

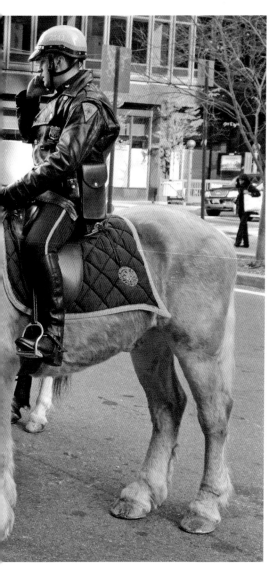

Greater Awareness
Despite the widespread
use of cars, New York's
Mounted Police Unit
is one of many still
used in cities. With a
growing awareness of the
welfare issues involved in
keeping animals in urban
environments, many
owners have switched
to more natural diets
and some keep their
horses unshod.

Work-Wear

The lead horse (middle) of this *troika* team wears a collar to distribute the load as it pulls. The structure that arches over the horse's head is a shaft-bow, to which the shafts of the sled are attached. Ear bonnets help muffle sounds and keep nervous horses calm; but here they may be used for decoration.

Young Horses

A new four-legged addition to the family is always exiting but, in a professional stable, foaling season is a busy time. A pregnant mare is said to 'be in foal' and horse-breeders will often try to time foaling so that all the youngsters are born in the spring. Growing up in a dark stable can cause illness and stifle a foal's natural development. Therefore, by ensuring that newborns have the opportunity to excercise outdoors, and enjoy the long, warm summer months, breeders are giving the foal the best start they can. Most foals are born at night. In the wild, this would have helped to keep the baby safe from the eyes and bellies of hungry predators until it was strong enough to run – which can take less than 24 hours. Mares and foals form strong bonds and the mother's presence is important in these early months to ensure that the youngster feels safe and learns 'horse etiquette', including how to interact with humans.

Horse mothers – called dams – are patient teachers, rewarding good behaviour with milk, encouraging whinnies and friendly nuzzles. As the foal grows, it quickly begins to learn from other members of the herd and horse-breeders appreciate that this has to happen slowly, with little outside human interference. After all, regardless of how skilled a breeder is, when it comes to learning those all-important life lessons, only a horse can teach a foal how to be a horse!

OPPOSITE:
Foal Facts
One-year-old members of the Family *Equidae* – donkeys, horses, mules, ponies and zebras – are all called foals. A mare can give birth at 18 months, but horse-breeders usually wait until she's fully grown, at around four years old, to mate her.

OPPOSITE:
Weights and Measures
On average, a newborn foal is 10 per cent of its dam's weight – but it grows quickly. Healthy foals suckle about 30 times per day, drinking 12–20 per cent of their body weight in milk.

LEFT TOP:
A Changing Diet
Mares can give birth once a year and, in the wild, they may allow their foals to nurse until a new foal is born. Foals naturally start 'sampling' grass after a few weeks but, in stables, they will be completely weaned off milk and on to solid food at 4–6 months.

LEFT BOTTOM:
Foal's First Meal
Immediately after birth, the dam will gently encourage her foal to feed. This first drink is called colostrum and it's loaded with antibodies to protect the newborn against disease.

A Protective Layer

Horses are born with hooves but, to protect the mother's womb from damage, these are covered in a rubbery layer known as a deciduous hoof capsule. This capsule looks like hundreds of finger-like fronds. The fronds quickly wear down as the foal starts to walk.

Growing Up

This foal is just nine days old. A fully grown adult Furioso-North Star horse averages 16 hands high. There's no agreed formula for determining a foal's adult height but, some horse-breeders say, that newborns are 60 per cent of their final size.

Easy to Spot

This newborn Appaloosa has a coat pattern that's known as a blanket. This covering of white spreads over the hips and, sometimes, covers the tail to the base of the neck. An Appaloosa's spots will always be the same colour as its horses' base coat.

A Little Horse Play

In their first few weeks of life, foals stick close to mum. When they play, it's in short bounds and trots – all the time keeping mum in their eyeline. At this age 'play' may also include nibbling mum's tail, which she patiently tolerates!

Strong Bonds

Within a couple of days, mother and foal have formed a close bond thanks to a process known as 'selective bonding'. New mothers can be very protective of their offspring and even well-behaved horses can be aggressive towards anyone who comes between her and her foal.

ABOVE:
Up and Away
Domesticated horses retain a vital survival trait from their wild ancestors: newborns become mobile very quickly. Foals start trying to stand within 10 minutes of being born. At the end of the first hour, they're on their feet. After an hour-and-a-half, they're walking – sometimes running.

OPPOSITE TOP:
Giving Birth
From start to finish, foaling can last for around eight hours, as the baby changes position inside the mare, ready to be born. The most obvious stage is when the placental sac breaks, expelling the amniotic fluid (called 'breaking water'). This typically takes anywhere from 15 minutes to two hours.

OPPOSITE BOTTOM:
First Steps
Foals can appear gawky and knock-kneed. This is due to loose ligaments in their legs, which tend to tighten as they grow. Occasionally foals are born with a condition called 'windswept legs', which looks as though the horse is being blown to one side. This requires specialist treatment.

ABOVE:

Colour Changes

This mother and her foal couldn't look more different from each other. However, grey horses – like this mare – often start life with dark coats. The gene that's responsible for the adult colouring will eventually turn the foal's coat a paler version of the colour it's born with.

RIGHT:

Totally Tobiano

Pied or piebald horses have white patches on a black base coat. This mother and her foal have a skewbald coat, in which white patches sit on a non-black coat. Here, the white patches are large and rounded. This pattern is known as 'tobiano'.

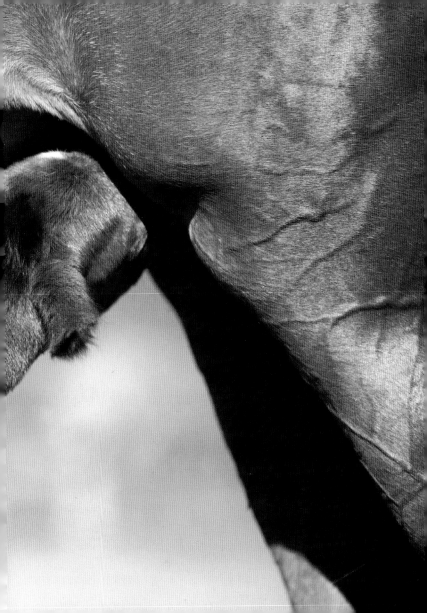

PREVIOUS PAGES:
Mamma's Milk
Mammary glands are what give mammals their name. In Latin, *mamma* means 'teat'. All female mammals produce milk for their children, which they feed to them via teats. This milk remains their main source of food until the youngsters are weaned and begin to eat solid food.

LEFT:
Play Mates
By the time they are three months old, foals are confident enough to spend at last half their day away from mum, feeding or playing with other foals. These foals (shown) are likely to be the same age but not related, as twins are very rare in the equine world.

OPPOSITE:

Learning the Ropes

A foal that's eating solid food, but is less than a year old, is known as a weanling. Horses reach puberty between two and three years of age. This is generally considered too young to start riding them, but the ideal age to begin more serious training.

ABOVE:

Precious Arrivals

This Suffolk Punch foal is a rare sight. The breed is considered to be critically endangered, with fewer than 500 registered in the world. In 2019, the Rare Breeds Survival Trust welcomed the arrival of a new filly foal, saying that she was 'rarer than a Panda'.

Wild & Feral Horses

For much of our history, human populations were tiny. It took until the early 1800s for the world's population to reach one billion. By the 1920s, it had already risen to two billion. Today, there are around 7.8 billion people on the planet and populations continue to grow.

Humans are voracious, and we use and consume resources with little regard for the other species that we share the planet with – especially land. The more of us there are, the more we consume and, increasingly, there are fewer wild spaces left. What survives in these tiny, natural enclaves tends to be those things that we can't use or no longer need. The horse is living proof of this.

In the distant past, wild horse populations roamed across Europe, Asia and North America. First people began to hunt them, then they domesticated them. So much so, that the world lost truly wild horses thousands of years ago. Today, breeds such as Przewalski's horse are as close as we can get to glimpsing a living, breathing wild equine – but even these ancient animals are really the descendants of the first horses to be domesticated, gone feral.

The good news is that a growing awareness of horses, as grazers and maintainers of natural eco-systems, means that many of these wonderful creatures are being returned to their ancient lands.

OPPOSITE:
Where the Bison Roam
In Paynes Prairie State Preserve in Florida visitors can see two species roaming wild, as they would have done in North America's distant past: bison and horses. The park originally started as a Spanish cattle ranch in the 1920s, and maintains small herds of both species.

Running Free

Created in the 1970s, the Parc naturel régional de Carmargue is a wild, windswept plain lying between the Rhone River and the Mediterranean Sea. Public access to the region is limited in order to maintain this hugely diverse animal paradise, where herds of Camargue horses still run free.

ABOVE TOP:
Managed Mustangs
The Divide Basin in Wyoming's Red Desert is home to both Mustangs and feral burro herds. Populations need to be carefully managed as the region can't support more than 100–230 horses. 'Excess' populations are regularly rounded up and offered for adoption.

ABOVE BOTTOM:
Desert Descendents
The Namib Desert is home to probably Africa's only remaining feral horses. Likely descended from escaped European cavalry horses, they live near Aus, Namibia, where there's a plentiful supply of fresh water.

OPPOSITE:
Welsh Wonders
A 2012 study found that Wales' Carneddau Ponies are 'genetically unique'. Four hundred years after they were saved from being culled, on the orders of Henry VIII, they remain an isolated herd, grazing the rugged mountain grasslands of Snowdonia.

Legal Protection
The Wyoming Bureau of Land Management oversees 16 horse management areas throughout America's cowboy state. In 1971, the Wild Free-Roaming Horses and Burros Act finally gave feral herds in the region legal protection and a safe place to roam, in recognition of the horse's place in American history.

To Purge or Preserve?

There's no doubting the appeal of these beautiful beasts but, all over the world, nature-lovers are arguing about the continued survival of feral horse herds. Some say that they should be culled, as they're neither wild nor native and, as such, shouldn't receive the same protection as other species.

LEFT:

Winter Gatherings

Feral horses roam free on northern Iceland's dramatic tabletop mountains for most of the year, but in autumn, farmers gather to round up, sort and corral their herds. The most famous of these sortings, *Laufskálarétt*, is on the last Saturday of September, and gives communities the chance to celebrate their horsey history together.

FOLLOWING PAGES:

Feral Instincts

Stampedes can be dangerous to both the animals involved and anything in their path. Although domestic horses can be docile, feral animals are highly strung and naturally nervous of any sudden movement or noise. Managing a herd's movements is one of the key skills a cowboy or cowgirl must learn.

OPPOSITE:

A Cool Solution

Feral horses have found all sorts of ingenious solutions to the problems of living outdoors. Horses may roll in the mud on a hot day to cool themselves down. The mud can also act like a barrier to deter biting insects and prevent sunburn.

ABOVE TOP:

Sharing is Caring

In cold, windy weather, there's nothing like snuggling up to stay warm. By huddling together, like this, horses reduce the body surface area that's exposed to the cold, while also sharing their own heat with younger or more vulnerable horses.

ABOVE BOTTOM:

It's Official!

This Canadian feral horse is known as the Sable Island pony. The breed is thought to date back to the late 1700s and analysis has shown that the population is now genetically unique from other North American herds.

PREVIOUS PAGES:
Vital Supplies
The average horse drinks
19–38 litres (40–80 pints)
of fresh water every day.
In the wild, they do get
some moisture from
grass, but while a hungry
horse can go without
food for 20–25 days,
a horse will die if
they're without water
for 3–4 days.

RIGHT:
Water Crossings
Feral horses don't
have to be taught to
swim because, in the
wild, crossing rivers
and swimming would
have been part of their
everyday experience.
Domestic breeds vary
from horse to horse, and
while some are confident
around water, others may
take a while to learn.

Tough Times

Winter can be hard for feral horses. Like all mammals, they keep themselves warm by 'burning' food as fuel. In colder temperatures, a body must work harder to stay warm. Generally horses need one per cent more food for each degree that the temperature drops below their core body temperature.

Picture Credits